Out of the Doctor's Bag

Copyright (c) 2011 Herbert L. Tanenbaum

All rights reserved. Printed in the U.S.A.

No part of this publication may be reproduced or transmitted in any form or by any means, electronic or mechanical, including photocopy, recording or any information storage and retrieval system now known or to be invented, without permission in writing from the publisher, except by a reviewer who wishes to quote brief passages in connection with a review written for inclusion in a magazine, newspaper or broadcast.

Published in the United States by
Beckham Publications Group, Inc.
P.O. Box 4066, Silver Spring, MD 20914

ISBN: 978-0-9833402-0-1

Out of the Doctor's Bag

*Anecdotes,
Tales, Stories, and Witticisms*

Herbert L. Tanenbaum, M.D.

PUBLICATIONS GROUP, INC.
Silver Spring

CONTENTS

PREFACE 1

PART ONE: **In the Beginning** 3
    HOW A CHICKEN CHANGED MY LIFE 4
    A COLORFUL LESSON 6
    A LESSON LEARNED 7
    BROWN OR BLUE 8
    YOU WANT TO DO, WHAT? 9
    A GIRL'S BEST FRIEND 10
    THERE MUST BE A REASON 11
    SURPRISE! 12

PART TWO: **Early Post-Graduate Years** 13
    HERE I AM AGAIN! 14
    KEEP THEM SMILING 15
    IT PAYS TO BE POOR 16
    I TOTALLY AGREE 18
    MY TREAT! 19
    NEXT COURSE, PLEASE 21
    FRESH SQUEEZED 22
    MEDIUM RARE, PLEASE 24
    DOG EAT DOG 25
    BOY, WAS I THIRSTY! 26
    FROM 'G' STRINGS TO HEART STRINGS 27

PART THREE: Practice Makes Perfect 29
- HERE'S MY CARD! 30
- JUST ONE MORE THING 31
- AS YE SOW, SO SHALL YE REAP! 32
- OURS IS NOT TO REASON WHY 34
- WHO IS PAYING THE BILL? 35
- IT DOESN'T LOOK LIKE TOMATO JUICE 36
- RX 37
- THE GOLDEN YEARS 38
- DIM SUM 39
- HAIL, BRITANNIA! 40
- WHAT'S FOR LUNCH? 41
- DOES MOTHER KNOW BEST? 42
- EMERGENCY 43
- THAT'S AMORE! 44
- IT COULD HAVE BEEN WORSE 46

PART FOUR: Communication 47
- INFORMED CONSENT 48
- YOU WANT ME TO SIGN, WHAT? 49
- MY, IT SURE IS HOT TODAY! 50
- ENGLISH, PLEASE! 51
- HOSPITAL JARGON 52
- WHO IS CALLING? 53
- WHAT DID YOU SAY? 54
- I CAN PLAINLY SEE 55
- SIMPLE ARITHMETIC 56
- WORDS OF WISDOM 57

PART FIVE: Relatively Speaking 59
- TAKE MY BAG, PLEASE! 60
- IT IS GOD'S TURN 62
- MOTHERS CAN TELL 63

Out of the Doctor's Bag

NOW, THAT'S FUNNY! 64
THEY GO ON SALE NEXT WEEK 65
IF I HAD MY WAY 66
THANK YOU VERY MUCH 67
A.A.D. (ALSO A DOCTOR) 68
A THIEF'S REWARD 69

PART SIX: Potpourri 71
YOURS OR MINE? 72
A PICTURE IS WORTH 1,000 73
GOD ACTS IN STRANGE WAYS 74
A DILEMMA 75
HER LUCKY DAY 76
FROM THE CRADLE TO THE GRAVE 77
TAXI, PLEASE! 78
WITH A PICKLE, OF COURSE! 79
WE NEVER GROW UP 80

PART SEVEN: Requiem 81
MALVERN MARTIN HAS PASSED AWAY 82
REQUIEM 83

ABOUT THE AUTHOR 85

PREFACE

Over the past 43 years, since graduating from medical school, I have worked in all phases of the medical disciplines; private practice, research, teaching, and administration. During these four decades, I have experienced many situations related to patient care. Some of these encounters have been filled with humor. And some are memorable for their tragic circumstances. But all are unforgettable and remarkably instructive for various reasons.

I have repeated these stories so many times to my colleagues and to students. And years after I have related these anecdotes, I often meet former students and physicians at medical meetings and chance encounters. They invariably tell me how they have always remembered an account I had told them so long ago.

Several have declared that the stories would bring delight have special meaning not ony to them, but also to the general reader if I collected them in book form.

So with the encouragement of my departed wife, Elaine Bresler Tanenbaum, I have pulled together these experiences to share with you. They reveal a great deal about not only the human spirit and what we determine to be important, but also about our use of language.

I am indebted to Elaine for her expertise in composition and her skills with manuscript editing. Finally, I would like to thank my patients, present and past, without whom these experiences would never have happened.

PART ONE:
IN THE BEGINNING

Herbert L. Tanenbaum

HOW A CHICKEN CHANGED MY LIFE

An individual's career is often determined by events outside of his control. These events occur, of course, against the background of one's lifes experiences and upbringing.

Let me explain how I chose a career in cardiology over the many disciplines available in the field of medicine.

As a child, I grew up living above my father's grocery store. Life was difficult. Everyone in the family worked long hours. Finding time for study during my college and medical school years was a real challenge.

One of my chores was to purchase live chickens from the market early on Saturday morning and bring them back to be sold, butchered and cleaned. Needless to say, this was a most unsavory task. The chickens would unload their excrement on the floor of my brother's 1931 Model A Ford. The mounds of sawdust and a thorough scrubbing only cleaned up the mess partially. The lingering odor was constantly in the car and in my mind. And the butchering and cleaning process was no enjoyable task.

As the years passed, the store was sold and I entered my postgraduate training years as a budding internist. My principal interest was in the field of nephrology or kidney disease, since I had worked with the artificial kidney during my residency.

After my residency years, I was accepted to the National Institutes of Health where I planned to continue training and research in the nephrology section. The director of the institute suggested that I spend time visiting the various laboratories to familiarize myself with the work being done before finally choosing where, and with whom, I wanted to work. Naturally, I wandered down to the kidney lab and introduced myself to the researchers in that unit.

Out of the Doctor's Bag

As I entered the kidney lab, a strange and familiar smell found its way to my nostrils. You guessed it! My God, the smell was that of chicken droppings! The experimental animal being studied was the chicken. After all those years of struggle and study, I would be back with the chickens for the next three years of my life.

No Way! I thought. I immediately began visiting other labs. In the cardiology section, I was greeted by a warm hello and words of encouragement by a world famous cardiologist. I decided that this is where I wanted to work.

Just consider. My entire life and career would have been different had the experimental animal in the kidney lab been a white rat.

A COLORFUL LESSON

Dr. J in medical school took threw out examination questions that often were out of the ordinary but were constructed to drive home an important lesson for the students. He also took a great deal of delight in collecting oddities.

A favorite question was to ask what color were the covers of different medical journals. He wanted to know if the students were going to the medical library and reading the journals.

A special exam question that remains in my memory was about a patient who complained of passing green urine. No one in our class could come up with the correct diagnosis. What in the world could cause the urine to be colored green? Perhaps it was a sign of some rare disease that we were not familiar with.

Dr. J's teaching point was to encourage the student to consider the most common probabilities when first approaching a diagnostic problem. The most common discoloration of the urine would be red, a result of passing blood. But he made the point that a not uncommon abnormality in men is color blindness with resulting difficulty in distinguishing the colors red and green. And so the correct answer was that the patient was color blind and was passing blood in the urine.

The lesson: If you hear hoof beats outside of your window, they are more likely from horses and not zebras!

A LESSON LEARNED

It was my first week of internship. I was a bright, well-trained recent medical school graduate eager to show off my knowledge to the full-time hospital staff, fellow interns, and to my new professors.

One of the hallmarks of a good intern is how he organizes, presents and analyzes a given patient's illness. After the presentation to the chief of service, the intern can further impress everyone with his knowledge of the literature that pertains to the patient's sickness.

Well, I worked up my patient from head to toe, reviewed all of the pertinent literature and prepared what I though was a polished presentation. With the chief of service and my fellow house staff at the patient's bedside, I started my report. "The patient is a 34-year-old black male who entered the hospital with the chief complaint… and so forth and so on."

I eagerly awaited the next phase during which time I would be quizzed about the diagnosis and discussion of his problem.

Unexpectedly, the chief invited me and the group out into the hallway. I was awaiting an accolade for a job well done.

The first comment that the chief of service made to me was, "Doctor, I could easily discern at the bedside that the patient was a black male!"

I never forgot that lesson! In my eagerness to appear knowledgeable in the subject matter and polished in my presentation, I presented the patient as an abstract case rather than as a human being at the bedside.

I have long forgotten the subsequent discussion of the disease, but the lesson of the day remains indelible. That experience and the teacher's remark is the essence of good education and training.

◆

BROWN OR BLUE

It is most important to perform a complete examination of the patient before making any conclusions. During my internship at a big city hospital, I was privileged to work with a very astute and brilliant resident and colleague. We used to share interesting medical challenges presented by different patients. Often, we would try to test the acuity of each other to see who could make the most accurate observations and diagnoses.

Early one morning, at approximately 2:00 A.M., I was awakened by my friend, who was on duty in the emergency room. He urged me to get dressed and come down to see a most interesting patient who was just admitted. With great reluctance, I arose, got dressed and dragged myself over the long corridors to the ER. Jim met me and introduced the patient. I was told to examine the patient's eyes with my ophthalmoscope. I did still being half asleep. After a long period of time, I confessed that I could not see any abnormalities with the patient's eyes.

With a smile, Jim admonished me, "Why don't you look first before using your scope? The patient happens to have a glass eye that you are trying to examine."

For this, I had to wake up at two in the morning!

YOU WANT TO DO WHAT?

While working in a city hospital environment, it is often impossible to obtain an adequate history from a confused or unconscious patient. Sometimes we can find the phone number of a relative in the patient's belongings. This situation came up one evening, when admitting an intoxicated and very ill man. I called his brother, whose phone number was in the patient's pocket.

Fortunately, I was able to contact the brother and tell him how seriously ill his brother appeared to be. I also inquired about any past significant medical history. The shouted reply that came across the phone was, "That no-good drunken S.O.B. brother of mine. I don't know and I don't want to know anything about him!" He slammed down the phone.

Later that week, in spite of all efforts, the patient died.

One of the more difficult tasks for a physician is to inform the family of the death of a family member and in many cases to request permission for a post-mortem examination of the body. Under the circumstances, I had to call the brother again. I asked for his permission to have an autopsy performed to establish the cause of death. His answer was loud and clear, "What? You mean you want to cut up my poor brother. He has suffered enough, poor soul. I absolutely refuse to allow such a procedure on my dear brother!"

Herbert L. Tanenbaum

A GIRL'S BEST FRIEND

It was a cold December night and three inches of snow lay on the ground. A taxi, from the Diamond Cab Company, screeched into the parking lot of the emergency room. The cab driver rushed in and screamed. "Help! There's a lady in the cab who's having a baby!"

We rushed out to the cab and what a scene to behold! Steam was coming out of all four windows from the warm amniotic fluid that had gushed from the mother-to-be. The expecting father was making deep tracks in the snow as he paced in circles around the cab. The cab driver was screaming to get the lady out of his cab where a mess had been created.

Well, mother was wedged firmly in the back seat since her weight approximated 250 pounds! The baby's head was beginning to show at the vaginal opening. Under the circumstances, the only thing I could do was to kneel on the front seat and face her. With great difficulty, I propped her legs up on top of the front seat.

In no time at all, I delivered a beautiful little girl. The cord was then cut and we managed to get the mother out of the cab, onto a stretcher and into the hospital.

The parents were happy, but the only consolation that the cab driver got was that the baby was going to be named, 'Diamond.'

Out of the Doctor's Bag

THERE MUST BE A REASON

One of the least regarded advances in medicine, as well as one of the most important, was the invention of the bedside commode.

Mr. P, a patient at the city hospital, had suffered a heart attack. In earlier days, a patient with a heart attack was kept in bed for several weeks. He was required to use a bedpan for evacuation. The effort required to get on and off a bedpan was greater than allowing the patient to get out of bed on to a chair. We would place the pan on the chair and this served as his commode.

At the city hospital, the bathroom for the entire ward was located down the hall. In spite of orders to the contrary, Mr. P would walk down the hall without help whenever he had to move his bowels. The nurses and doctors reprimanded him for this daily activity which was against orders.

Finally, Mr. P, with an embarrassing blush on his face, explained. "Look, he said, the good Lord endowed me with a large masculine organ. If you felt your family jewels hanging down into the bedpan and its contents, you would walk down the hall too!"

The new order read, "Mr. P may now have bathroom privileges"!

SURPRISE!

Not only do little children have big ears and often overhear conversations, but adults do the same. One must be careful about what seems an aside remark.

During the clinical years of medical school, the student spends time in a gynecological clinic where she learns, under supervision, how to perform a pelvic exam. I anxiously awaited the chief resident's instructions.

Our patient was up in stirrups and the vaginal speculum tool was warmed and carefully inserted to show the cervical part of the uterus. At the end of the cervix, a small slit is the opening of the uterus.

It was difficult to see the organ at first and the instructor repeatedly described and tried to point out the opening for the students to recognize. "Don't you guys see it? There, the little *dimple* on the cervix."

The patient, having overhead the remark, sat up suddenly with a smile. "My gosh, Doctors, I didn't know I had a dimple on my *twat*!"

PART TWO:
EARLY POST-GRADUATE YEARS

HERE I AM AGAIN!

Mr. W was a patient at a large city hospital where I served my internship. He had a rare congenital neurological abnormality and provided an excellent teaching case for the medical students and house staff. Mr. W loved the attention, the free hospital room and board, and the nurses.

After a prolonged hospital stay, it was time for him to be released. He refused! Only with help from the administration and social service were we able to discharge him from the hospital. As he left the unit, he waved goodbye to the staff and insisted, "I'll be back!"

Would you believe that after discharge, Mr. W went down to the state capitol? He lowered his trousers and defecated on the steps! He appeared confused and was immediately taken by the police to the hospital emergency room and reappeared on our unit. If the hospital admission was a repeat admission within a one-year period, the patient is returned to the same floor and service where he had been previously treated.

After being put into his bed, he suddenly cleared mentally and waved. "Hi guys, I told you I would be back!"

KEEP THEM SMILING

The art of medicine assumes many forms. Often there is no scientific basis for the practice of this art, only a hunch and deep concern for the emotional well-being of a patient.

Many years ago, a colleague was stricken by an illness characterized by high fever, enlarged lymph nodes and weight loss. His white blood count was markedly abnormal.

After being examined by a well-known hematologist from a highly academic medical school, Sam was diagnosed as having acute leukemia. In those days, no treatment was known and my physician friend was aware of this fact.

Upon being informed of the diagnosis, Sam became severely depressed and morose with periods of audible weeping. Psychiatric counselling didn't help. I suggested that he get another opinion, although with little hope of any different diagnosis or eventual outcome.

Dr. H was an old country doctor, although head of the department of medicine at a lesser known medical school. He listened patiently to Sam and examined him with hope and confidence in his demeanor.

After the examination, Dr. H, with his usual poor grammar and Southern accent, said, "Sam, you ain't got no leukemia. In spite of the laboratory tests, I think you have infectious mononucleosis (a relatively benign disease). I think you are gonna get better. Stop your frettin'."

Outside, in the hallway, we asked Dr. H how he came to that conclusion in spite of the lack of laboratory evidence for the diagnosis of mono. He smiled, "I guess it's just a hunch. I might be wrong, I might be right, but look in that room. He's smiling for the first time in weeks!" Seven days later, Sam's blood test for mono, was positive!

Herbert L. Tanenbaum

IT PAYS TO BE POOR

It might be difficult to believe that growing up in a poor crowded neighborhood would have some advantages. One benefit is to be exposed to several communicable diseases with low enough virulence to confer immunity to the exposed person and not be severe enough to manifest overt infections with their dire consequences.

As a resident in a busy city hospital, my duties included rotating through the infectious disease section. That summer of 1954, the city was hit with a serious epidemic of poliomyelitis. Patients would walk into the emergency room and within twelve hours would become completely paralyzed and had to be placed in the artificial lung to sustain life. The year before my rotation, another resident had been infected from a patient he cared for. The resident subsequently died.

One evening, I admitted a young pregnant woman who was near her delivery time. Her polio infection was of the worse possible kind, involving the brain stem. The artificial iron lung respirator was required. Her prognosis was essentially hopeless. However, there was the distinct possibility that we could deliver her infant with a good chance for survival. And the baby would not be infected.

That night, I slept on the ward on a small couch. If she came close to expiring, we were ready to do an immediate Caesarean section.

Some of the symptoms of polio are headache, fatigue and a stiff neck. After working nearly 24 hours without sleep and lying on a small couch, I awoke with these symptoms and saw the writing on the wall. My God! I've been exposed to some of the most severe cases of polio, I have the symptoms that the resident the year before had died from.

With trepidation, I continued to work and carry out my duties. Time passed and to my good fortune, nothing happened to me. There is no doubt in my mind that exposure to the disease, as a child growing up in the crowded poverty-type neighborhood gave me a level of immunity. Sometimes it pays to be poor!

Herbert L. Tanenbaum

I TOTALLY AGREE

In my previous story, I made reference to admitting a young pregnant woman at term with acute bulbar poliomyelitis. We realized that she would not survive. Should we allow her to deliver in a normal manner or perform an urgent Caesarean section at high risk to both mother and child?

The professor of obstetrics at a highly respected medical school was consulted. His opinion was to go ahead with the C-Section. Since as I was a medical resident on a different medical school's service, I was obliged to consult with my medical department chief. He was an old country doctor who had years of experience, a keen intuitive mind, and was a superb teacher.

Dr. H knew how hard I had been working that month on the polio unit. After examining the patient, his years of experience and insight helped him to come to a different opinion than the other consultant.

Dr. H took me out into the conference room. As a good teacher, he wanted me to make the decision and hopefully add to my self esteem. "Dr. T," he said as he shook his head side to side in a negative manner. "You don't want to operate on that poor lady, do you?" The phrasing of the question and his negative head motion allowed me to reply.

"No, Sir, I do not." Now he shook his head in a positive manner.

"I agree with you one hundred percent. I think she will deliver within 24 hours. We will probably lose the mother in a few days, but we will have a better chance to get a normal baby."

Dr. H had made the decision, but gave me the dignity of appearing to have made it. Twenty-four hours after that, we delivered a beautiful healthy little girl. The mother expired two days later.

MY TREAT!

While working as a resident physician in New Orleans, I was able to use my vacation time to serve as a ship's doctor for two weeks. Although the ship was a freighter, she carried 50 passengers and required a physician to be on board. The voyage was great fun and the dining terrific, especially after months of city hospital food.

As a ship's officer, I socialized with both the passengers and crew. One of my duties was to have lunch with the crew just prior to arriving at a port of call. I would place a box of condoms on the table and urge the crew to use them. Invariably, three to five days after setting sail again, I would diagnose and have to treat at least six cases of venereal disease, in spite of my instructions and condom handouts.

Another duty assigned to me was to socialize with the passengers. I was given a fifteen dollar bar credit to help entertain the guests. For a poor medical resident with little income, this was great. I would invite different passengers into the bar, order drinks and tell Mike, the bartender, to put them on my account. In contrast to my financial status, the passengers, for the most part, were quite wealthy.

When we arrived at different ports, the guests for whom I bought drinks the previous evening, would insist on taking me out to lunch, especially since they knew of the meagre pay I received as a resident at the city hospital. The lunches were quite lavish at luxurious hotels in each port.

At the end of the cruise, I approached Mike the bar-tender and asked him how much I owed on my bar bill. I was certain that I had exceeded the fifteen dollar credit by a substantial amount.

"Doc," Mike replied, "you have a credit balance of $14. I put all of your charges on the passengers' bills. They had so many drinks over the past few weeks that they wouldn't know the difference anyway, and besides, they could well afford them."

Can I buy you a drink?

NEXT COURSE, PLEASE

During my two weeks experience as a ship's doctor, I never missed a meal. The contrast between the delicious food served on the cruise with the tasteless dining at the hospital was overwhelming.

During the trip, we experienced a severe storm at sea with windows blown out and the ship listing from side to side. Everyone, crew and passengers alike, were sea-sick with marked gastrointestinal distress. I was busy giving injections all day long. Fortunately, I am very resistant to motion sickness and felt no ill effects from the storm.

That evening, I was the only one to make it to the dining room. The edges of the tables were raised to prevent the dishes from sliding off as the ship rocked. The cook came out of the kitchen wearing a sallow green complexion on his face and said, "Are you kidding, Doc. How are you able to eat?" I explained that I felt fine and quite hungry. I knew that in a few days I would be back to the horrible hospital fare.

The cook then went back to the kitchen and brought out what must have been a twenty pound turkey with all the trimmings. "Here, help yourself!," he muttered as he rushed to the bathroom.

At this point, there was one major problem I faced. I had to spear the turkey as it slid from one side of the table to the other with each roll of the ship. Guess who won the duel?

FRESH SQUEEZED

Mishaps can occur in business, industry or in medical practice. Unfortunately, in today's world, they often result in the statement, "My lawyer will hear about this in the morning!"

In past years, if no injury resulted from the error, patients accepted the accidental event as one of those things that happens and they would thank goodness that they were not harmed.

Two of these experiences come to mind during my training. The first occurred in the hospital after a patient received an unmatched blood transfusion. A reaction immediately followed, characterized by a skin rash and kidney shutdown that lasted one day. She suffered no residual ill effects. Her only comment after the incident was, "Thank goodness this happened to me while I was in the hospital! I don't know what I would have done if I were at home."

The second event, at a different hospital, concerned a patient who was admitted with severe dehydration. In those days, the intravenous fluids were made up in large sterile flasks at the hospital.

The patient was quite alert and could take additional fluids by mouth. She said that she loved lemonade. One of the hospital aides opened up a flask of glucose, added some more sugar and squeezed some lemons into the solution. The flask was placed by the patient's bedside for her to drink and enjoy.

That evening, while the patient was asleep, another aide noted that the intravenous fluid infusing into her arm vein was running out. The aide, by accident, replaced the completed infusion with the lemonade flask by the bedside.

The next morning on rounds, lemon seeds were noted in the fluid filter trap. No ill effects ensued.

I can imagine the patient telling her friends after discharge, "When they tell you at the hospital to drink lemonade, you *better drink lemonade.*"

MEDIUM RARE, PLEASE

Food that is served to the resident staff of a city hospital is a far cry from that of a gourmet restaurant, to say the least. There was never a choice of how well-done the meat was to be cooked nor what was being served. You ate what was put in front of you or remained hungry until you were off duty.

One of the chief residents, Dr. M, seemed to always approach the dining room with an optimistic smile on his face. He would tell the waitress that Dr. M was being served and to please relate that fact to the kitchen. Out came a better cut of meat, tender and medium rare, as he liked it cooked. The other residents later learned that the cook was a good friend and a patient of Dr. M.

Later in the year, Dr. M went away for a week's vacation. The house staff came to the dining room at the regular time and we were served our cold soup and questionable appetizer. When it came time for the entrée, the cook suddenly ran out of the kitchen. In a loud voice he yelled, "What's going on here? There are fifteen guys who claim that they are Dr. M."

Well, it was worth the try.

DOG EAT DOG

One of the negative aspects of medical education is the fierce competition that is developed. This usually occurs during the pre-med college years when students vie for the limited medical school admissions. The pressure lessens as the student enters the post-graduate stage of his training. During my years of training, there was a great variation in the degree of competition in different parts of the country. It seemed to be most intense in areas like New York City and Boston.

One evening, during my cardiac fellowship in Bethesda, Maryland, a highly respected professor was conducting a seminar at another hospital across town. Fortunately, I was not on call that night and planned to attend. One of my colleagues who was on call was very disappointed to be missing the conference. We were very close friends and I reassured him that I would take detailed notes and share them with him.

He smiled, thanked me and appeared extremely grateful. His over enthusiastic response raised my curiosity. "Gene, wouldn't your classmates in New York have done the same for you under these circumstances?"

His reply was, "They certainly would take notes for me. However, they would give me different notes!"

So much for life in the big city!

BOY, WAS I THIRSTY!

One of my colleagues tells of an experience he had with an elderly female patient admitted to the emergency room. She was brought into the hospital and with very general complaints. The patient was judged by the admitting doctor not to be in any acute distress. The ER was very crowded and busy so that the elderly lady had to wait for further evaluation and tests. During this her wait, she complained of excessive thirst and kept asking for a glass of water. There was no response to her request. Again she cried out, "Can someone get me a glass of water, please?" Again, no response.

Suddenly, the patient experienced an irregular rhythm to her heart beat. She then went into cardiac arrest. Fortunately, this was witnessed by a physician and a code blue emergency was called. She was successfully resuscitated. As the nurses were propping her up to swallow some medication with a glass of water, she unexpectedly exclaimed, "My goodness, you almost have to die to get a glass of water in this hospital!"

FROM "G" STRINGS TO HEART STRINGS

After I completed my residency at the National Institutes of Health and joined the Washington Hospital Center staff, I was asked to supervise the new cardiac lab and develop an equipment list.

We were just entering the age of good measurement of the physiological determination of cardiac events. We needed new equipment to improve the diagnosis and treatment of heart disease. I didn't know what to charge for my services which included setting up and supervising the lab, so I asked my fiancé, who later became my wife, and she suggested that I charge $100. So I did.

We had to be very creative in the beginning, because equipment was crude and funds were scarce. When it was time to perform catheterizations to obtain measurements of key cardiac parameters, we made our own catheters. I would take plastic tubing made in Sweden, put the tubes in boiling water and shape them to the desired configuration.

When we needed wires for arterial guides, I used guitar "G" strings that I bought from a local music store. After I used a string twice, I had to throw it out. When I started buying twelve of the "G" strings at a time, the salesman commented, "You must play a mean guitar."

PART THREE:
PRACTICE MAKES PERFECT

Herbert L. Tanenbaum

HERE'S MY CARD!

A young doctor learns many practical lessons in the early years of his career. When I first entered practice, I became active in several fraternal organizations, hoping to meet potential patients. At meetings of these groups, the young new doctor is often beset upon by well-meaning new acquaintances who try to get some free medical advice.

Once, a well-to-do member approached me and unloaded all of his medical woes upon me. He recounted how he spent a great deal of time, money and some discomfort while being worked up for the finding of "blood in his stool." The examination took place at a well known New York hospital. No abnormality was found and he returned to his home.

The problem reoccurred and again he underwent testing, of a similar nature, at a local medical school hospital. Once more, no diagnosis was offered. Out of curiosity, I questioned him as to what he meant by "blood in the stool?" His description of the discoloration was that of a mahogany color rather than fresh blood or dark, tarry old blood. I asked about his dietary habits and discovered that he loved to eat borsch, (beet soup.) I suggested that there may be a relationship of his discolored stools to his ingestion of beets. I told him to eliminate borscht from his diet for a week.

As it turned out, I was correct about the cause of his problem. I expected to acquire a new patient after this experience. I don't remember even getting a, 'thank you.'

From that time on, all medical questions directed to me, were answered by, "That's an interesting problem. Here is my professional card. If you wish, you may make an appointment to see me in my office."

JUST ONE MORE THING

I had just started my medical practice and was trying to rush to the office early one morning. Before leaving, I received a phone call from the mother of a very close friend with whom I grew up. "Ralph is in bed with a very bad cold. Would you come to our house and see him this morning?"

I figured it was on my way down town to the office and should not take very long. In those days, all of us were just starting out in our professions and jobs and no charge was ever made for services to our close friends.

Mrs. D, Ralph's mother, met me at the door and escorted me to the bedroom. I examined my friend, diagnosed the respiratory illness and wrote some prescriptions. As I was leaving the house, Mrs. D ran after me. "Herbie, (after all, she knew me long before I became Dr. T), will you please run down to the drug store and fill the prescriptions?"

What could I say? "Yes, Ma'am!" I though to myself, "So I'll be a little late."

I started to depart once more. Again I was called back. "While you are at the drug store, I need a few things from the grocery store next door. Here is the list." I once more agreed and politely replied, "Yes, Mrs. D." One step out of the door and a final, "Herbie, the laundry is on the same block; here is the ticket."

Well, after all, that's what friends are for!

Herbert L. Tanenbaum

AS YE SOW, SO SHALL YE REAP!

A constant reminder of the horror that man can inflict upon another human being is the observation of concentration camp numbers tattooed on a person's arm. One of several of my patients survived Hitler's Hell and lived to tell the story.

In pre-war Germany, Mr. H was a college-educated gentleman and a bookbinder. He was kindly and well liked. Each Sabbath eve, a poor, elderly man passed his shop and Mr. M would give him a loaf of *challah* bread for the Sabbath.

Along came the war and my patient was incarcerated in a concentration camp. His foot was badly mangled and he was near starvation and death. A German officer who knew him in college asked if he might help in any way. Mr. H replied, "I'm going to die. Please let me see the commandant." Mr. H. was dragged into the commandant's office on his abdomen. He was spit upon and was surprisingly told to leave the camp. The authorities were certain that Mr. H would not survive for more than a half a day, considering his physical condition and the cold winter weather.

With nothing but hope, a will to survive and sheer determination, Mr. H made his way out of Germany and eventually travelled to the Far East where his sister had also made her escape.

After regaining some strength, he worked in the underground and aided Canadian pilots who were downed in the area.

By this time, he was infected with diffuse tuberculosis. The Canadians took him back to Canada for treatment and his eventual recovery.

After the war, Mr. H came to the United States and eventually became my patient.

To complete the story, Mr. H accidentally met the gentleman he had befriended with bread before the war. The son of this gentleman was a successful developer and builder in the local area. For my patient's acts of kindness, at the request of the developer's father, Mr. H was given a new home to live in.

"The mills of the gods grind slowly, but they grind exceedingly fine!"

OURS IS NOT TO REASON WHY

All of us wonder at times whether events are preordained or directed by advice from men wiser than we. A fine gentleman who recently married one of my patients consulted me for the first time after the urging of his new wife. Both had lost their spouses and were a perfect match for each other at their stage of life.

Mr. J, originally had reservations about getting married again. He was advised by a brilliant, almost mystical rabbi whom he had known for many years. The rabbi, after being informed of the lady's background and the type of person the future bride was, recommended that they certainly should marry. "A man is not a complete person until he is joined in marriage," was his advice. "But remember, before getting married, keep both eyes open. After you are married, you must close one eye."

Mr. J's medical history was quite benign and he offered no complaints about his health. The only reason he came to my office was because of the insistence of his new wife.

At the time of the examination, I recorded his blood pressure to be 240/120. High blood pressure of this degree is the silent killer leading to strokes, heart attacks and kidney failure. With a regimen of proper medication, his blood pressure was nicely controlled.

Who had the mystical power to have saved his life—the rabbi, his wife or both?

WHO IS PAYING THE BILL?

Those of us who have children are constantly irritated when the kids leave the lights on when they go to another room in the house. When they come home from school or on holidays, it seems that every light in the house is left burning wherever they may have been. Maybe it's a generation gap and our parents did a better job in training us than we are doing.

These thoughts come to mind on several occasions in my office. I can sometimes gather information about my patient's socioeconomic status, behavioral attitudes, and more, by merely observing their dress and demeanor. One observation that brings a smile to my face is when I notice that a minority of patients, who upon getting dressed after their examination, leave the examining room and always turn off the lights.

I can hear their parents' admonition now. "When you have to pay the electric bill, then you will remember to turn off the lights!"

Herbert L. Tanenbaum

IT DOESN'T LOOK LIKE TOMATO JUICE

One of the more humorous encounters in my medical practice involved an elderly patient who came in for her routine diabetic checkup. The evaluation always included a complete urinalysis. The patient brought in her usual empty vitamin bottle filled with her amber A.M. specimen.

When the examination was completed, the patient departed and awaited my telephone call to discuss the results of her examination and laboratory findings. My nurse checked the patient's specimen and noted a strong four-plus glucose reaction and informed me.

I immediately called the patient to reprimand her for not following her diet. Before I could complete a sentence, she interrupted me and said, "Doctor, I forgot to bring in my urine specimen this morning."

I replied, "But Mrs. G, you left it in your usual place on the counter in your old vitamin bottle."

"Doctor, that was my apple juice which I always drink after my blood is taken. I just love apple juice!"

Out of the Doctor's Bag

RX

Whenever a physician prescribes a medication, he usually tells the patient the name of the medication, the reason for which it is being prescribed, and any possible side effects that might be experienced. If the pills have been prescribed by another physician, I always ask for details what he is taking and the results of the treatment. This information can often be a learning experience for me also.

Mrs. P was seeing a neurologist for her problems with progressive memory loss. She was given a prescription with explicit instructions about the medication and how to use it.

After taking the medication for several months, she consulted me for her routine checkup. During the examination, I asked her, "Mrs. P, what medication have you been taking for your memory that was prescribed by the neurologist?"

She looked up at me and replied, "You know doctor, I forgot the name of the pills!"

So much for modern pharmacology!

Herbert L. Tanenbaum

THE GOLDEN YEARS

The later years of your life are often referred to as the "golden years." To many people, this terminology is far from the truth. The onset of arthritis, failing vision, decreased mobility, decreased sexual function and frequent visits to the doctor hardly translate to golden years.

One afternoon, I examined a very proper, well-educated and prim elderly lady. She was dressed in a calico cotton dress, sturdy black-laced shoes and wore a tiny black hat with a pink rose upon her closely curled gray locks. She suffered from advanced osteoarthritis. Mrs. R reminded me of an old school teacher or grandmother who has strict standards of behavior and speech.

During the examination, she suddenly exclaimed with a loud voice, "Doctor, anybody who says these fucking years are golden, are full of shit."

I don't think her feelings could have been expressed more succinctly.

DIM SUM

It is said that we are made up of what we eat. This maxim of course would not hold true if the food consumed was not digested and absorbed. Accordingly, I always make some subtle remarks when examining a patient's large intestine by means of a procto-sigmoidoscopic examination.

One Sunday, my wife and I were dining out at a local Chinese restaurant. I noticed one of my patients leaving as we were coming in. He did not see me in the crowded lobby.

The following day, he appeared at the office for his scheduled annual physical examination which included the large bowel study described above. He mounted the table and assumed the usual position on his left side in preparation for the exam. I reassured him and proceeded to pass the instrument into the rectum. Half way through the exam, I exclaimed, "John, I see that you like Chinese food."

He turned to me with a surprised look. "How did you know that?"

"In fact," I replied, "I can tell you like the cooking at the Peking Restaurant!" With that remark, he nearly fell off the table.

A similar incident involved a patient on a Monday morning. I noted undigested poppy seeds on the surface of the bowel. It did not take much reasoning to explain that they came from the ingestion of a bagel with poppy seeds the day before. He smiled at my assessment.

At times, my patients must think that I am some sort of medical Sherlock Homes. At any rate, they are more relaxed by my remarks when having this somewhat uncomfortable examination.

HAIL, BRITANNIA!

There are many ways to relax when confronted by an unpleasant experience. You could try to fill your mind with happy thoughts or think of what you would like for dinner. You might recall a funny story or a pleasant melody.

Mr. G, a fine, well-spoken Englishman with a thick British accent, was about to have a proctoscopic examination. I reassured him that the procedure would not be difficult and explained what would occur.

He quietly assumed the position on his elbows and knees while I prepared the instruments. After I carefully inserted the proctoscope into his rectum, he suddenly started to sing, "God Save the Queen" to the tune of "My Country tis of Thee," of course. He seemed relaxed, and I continued to insert the scope farther up the colon. As the scope was advanced, his singing became louder in volume and faster in tempo. Far be it for me to interrupt the means by which he relaxed.

Near the end of the examination, the pitch and tempo were so pronounced that my nurse rushed into the room to see what was happening.

We were both astonished and wondered whether the British flag was about to be raised again on American soil!

Out of the Doctor's Bag

WHAT'S FOR LUNCH?

A very well-known diplomat and statesman patient of mine was undergoing his annual physical. It included a routine examination of the rectum and sigmoid colon by means of proto-sigmoidoscopy.

Just prior to the exam, Mr. K had related to me how he had just returned from a diplomatic mission to the Middle East. He attended a conference which took place in the great halls of Egypt. There was only one pause, and that was for lunch. Well, that day, lunch included a so-called delicacy, a sheep's eye. My patient would rather have had a corned beef sandwich, but not wanting to insult the host, he ate the delicacy.

Returning home, he came into my office for his scheduled appointment. During a proctoscopic examination I often make remarks, sometimes humorous, to relax my patient. In this instance, I advanced the instrument up the colon and suddenly exclaimed. "My gosh, Mr. K, guess what? I'm looking through the scope and to my surprise, another eye is looking back to me!" My patient was quite amused by my remark, laughed and was more relaxed for the remainder of the examination.

The following week, he was back in the Middle East for another round of conferences. In the late morning, during one of the sessions, which was quite drawn out, his mind wandered as he thought about lunch. What if it were sheep's eyes again? The remark I had made during the previous week's examination crossed his mind, and he started to laugh. The other conferees gave him a stern look as if to ask, "What is so funny about these serious negotiations?" I don't know how he was able to explain his laughter.

Little did I know how a chance remark in my examining room might have led to an international incident.

Herbert L. Tanenbaum

DOES MOTHER KNOW BEST?

When taking a medical history from a patient, physicians often get incomplete or unusual answers to questions. When I reviewed the family history of one of my patients. I asked, "What did your mother die from?"

"Oh, she passed away several years ago, but I don't think she died of anything serious."

Another odd answer sometimes happens when asking patients what medication they are taking. Their response usually includes only prescription drugs, but not over-the-counter medications like aspirin or vitamins.

Miss K was a young dental nurse who was troubled by severe neck pains for several months. Her examination showed no abnormalities. In addition, she had seen several orthopedic and neurosurgical specialists to no avail. I specifically asked her about over-the-counter medicines or vitamins she was taking. She told me that her mother, who was living in another state, was a great believer in vitamins. In fact, she would send her daughter large quantities of multi-vitamins that she purchased from mail order supply houses. I asked her to bring the vitamins to the office.

When I examined the vitamin bottles, I noted she was taking an extremely high dose of Vitamin A. Her symptoms fitted those that can occur with Vitamin A intoxication. After discontinuing the mega doses of Vitamin A that she was consuming, her symptoms cleared.

Sometimes, mothers are not always right!

EMERGENCY

It was a late Friday afternoon when I received a frantic call from a patient. He moaned, groaned and complained of severe pain and swelling of his right large toe. I was already late for hospital rounds, but I realized that the patient was in excruciating pain and needed immediate relief.

So I agreed to rearrange my schedule and wait in the office until he could come in to be examined.

When he arrived and was examined, it was clear that the diagnosis was indeed acute gout. I reassured him and prescribed some medication that usually brings early and welcome relief within 24 hours. In addition, the cost of the medication was relatively inexpensive. He thanked me, but hesitated.

The patient turned to me and quietly asked if he could wait until Monday to get the prescription filled. He explained that his nephew was a pharmacist and would give him a reduced price for the prescription on Monday, three days later, when his nephew would return to work.

I nodded in amazement as he limped out of the office.

THAT'S AMORE!

Many case histories in a physician's experience would make a fascinating TV drama or movie. Once I was on the teaching service of a large inner-city hospital. One night a patient was brought into the emergency room in a confused and combative state. He appeared to be in a drunken stupor. No history was available from the young woman accompanying him because she spoke only Italian. His physical examination, laboratory and X-ray studies didn't reveal enough for us. So a spinal tap was clearly necessary. In those days the sophisticated techniques of a CT scan and an MRI of the head were not available.

We chose to follow the patient closely in spite of the negative findings. After he was admitted to the hospital, the young lady refused to leave his bedside. She even slugged a hospital guard who tried to move her away. That night, the patient's pulse rate began to fall and he showed signs of increased pressure in the brain. I urged the attending neurosurgeon to operate to relieve the pressure. After several hours, the patient was taken to the operating room at my insistence. Blood shot out under pressure when burr holes were made on both sides of his skull, indicating bilateral subdural hemorrhages.

Post operatively, the patient did poorly with falling blood pressure readings and breathing problems. A shock-like state ensued. All supportive life-sustaining measures were instituted. After two weeks of these extraordinary measures, the chief resident suggested that we were faced with a patient who would very likely not recover. I refused to give up our efforts. The young lady who accompanied him to the hospital waited at his bedside.

As time passed, the patient made a miraculous recovery and was left with a mild residual right-sided weakness and a moderate speech defect. At this point, we had learned that the patient was a brilliant member of the cultural section of the Italian Embassy and a world's expert on Michelangelo. Three months prior to his admission to the hospital, he had moved some statuary from the basement and struck his head against the base of a statue. This accident caused a slowly developing bleed on the surface of the brain that was unable to be diagnosed initially.

The young lady turned out to be a helper at his residence. After discharge from the hospital, my wife and I were invited to his home for a magnificent Italian dinner prepared by the young lady. During the dinner, my wife remarked to me that the young lady seemed to be very much in love with my patient. I accused my wife of being an incurable romantic.

Two months later, we were invited to the wedding of the devoted housekeeper to her secret love and adored diplomat!

IT COULD HAVE BEEN WORSE

Shortly after going into practice, I unfortunately was injured in a serious automobile accident. My scalp was badly lacerated and I required hospitalization. My head was tightly bandaged and blood was slowly oozing under the gauze. I was being prepared for the operating room for the suturing of my head wounds.

A friend and colleague made a courtesy visit to my room. He took one look at me and exclaimed, "My gosh, Herb, you really were injured, but it could have been worse!"

I appreciated his visit and concern and replied, "You are right, Jack, I could have been killed."

With a partial smile on his face, he interrupted, "No, I meant, it could have been me."

I still don't know whether he was trying to make me feel better by his remark or was really serious. At any rate, now you know how physicians try to cheer each other up!

PART FOUR:
COMMUNICATION

INFORMED CONSENT

Before the flood of medical malpractice suits, many of which turn out to be groundless, physicians could practice the art of medicine without the worry that their judgments would be legally questioned.

My mother, at the age of 55 was an industrious, hard-working woman who rarely rested from toiling in her grocery store, keeping house, and raising her family. One weekend, she was seized with severe abdominal pain, vomiting and dehydration. Her skin color became deeply jaundiced.

It was late Saturday night when a well-known surgeon was called in by her family physician. The surgical professor made a house call that late weekend evening to examine my mother. Dr. H knew the type of woman he was dealing with and what had to be done to handle the situation. "Tessie", he said, "you need an emergency operation to remove a dangerously infected gall bladder before it perforates."

However, as expected, Mom would under no circumstances leave her home, store and responsibilities. The grocery had to be opened early the next morning.

All of us were exasperated. Finally Dr. H screamed in a loud commanding voice, "I don't care what you want! You are going to the hospital right now with me, and I am going to operate on you tonight!" He even helped carry her down to his car.

In two hours, she was in the operating room where an early perforated, infected gall bladder was successfully removed. She made a recovery without complications and survived for another 39 years after that life-threatening illness.

Now that's what I call the art of medicine, even without informed consent.

YOU WANT ME TO SIGN WHAT?

The laws pertaining to informed consent were passed to enable the patient to be fully informed about the possible risks and consequences of a given procedure. However, there may be a down side to the regulation, often to the detriment of the patient.

Miss B was a middle-aged, unmarried lady with a history of recurrent episodes of depression. She had been seen by several psychiatrists who had prescribed numerous different anti-depressant medications. Psychotherapy was not of use and even electroshock treatment was considered.

One of her principal problems was that she had a poor self-image. To make matters worse, her facial features showed signs of early aging with numerous wrinkles and bags under her eyes. She certainly would benefit from a simple face lift operation. This low-risk procedure would have greatly improved her ego, appearance and self-esteem, and afford a definite amelioration of her depression.

She consulted with a very competent plastic surgeon. He agreed that she would be an excellent candidate for a face lift, with a beautiful anticipated result. However, before scheduling her for the simple out-patient procedure, by law, he had to list all the possible complications from the operation.

These included death from the anesthesia, infection and disruption of the sutures, and more. All of these problems rarely ever happen. What a list to present to a depressed patient!

Miss B listened to the surgeon's obligatory remarks, turned around and walked out of his office. Her depression remains, as well as her wrinkles.

So much for the progress of informed consent under the law.

MY, IT SURE IS HOT TODAY!

Words can sometimes be deceiving when overheard. Occasionally, this deception can lead to an embarrassing situation.

A patient complained to me, during her examination, that an elderly couple in the waiting room was using foul language. After the patient departed, the elderly couple came into my office, and I was obliged to ask about the charge.

It turned out that the office was quite uncomfortable during a particularly hot summer day. The air conditioning was also not functioning well. The wife, in this hot environment, turned to her husband and requested that he "fan her with his newspaper."

Unfortunately, the couple spoke very little English. The Yiddish (their primary language) word for fan is *fuch*. She was constantly requesting her husband to *fuch* her in the waiting room.

ENGLISH, PLEASE!

Proper communication between the physician and the patient is of great consequence. We try our best to relate to patients even when there are language barriers.

An elderly gentleman was referred to me by a retiring physician. The patient's command of the English language was not very good. It was quite difficult for him to describe his medical history and current complications to me. As a result, he appeared quite uncomfortable at this first visit and was incomplete in describing his medical problems. I was fully aware of his difficulties with communication and also understood that his primary language was Yiddish.

Now, my understanding of Yiddish is only fair and my ability to speak the language even less so. However, in light of the circumstances, I was willing to make a stab at it. My hope was that he would be more comfortable and express his problems more easily.

Of course, this approach resulted in a strain on my part as I had to struggle to remember my limited Yiddish vocabulary and the words that would be pertinent to a medical history. In addition, this added effort required a great deal more time.

Mr. B's responses, now in Yiddish, were clear, less inhibited and he exhibited a much more relaxed manner, in spite of my perspiration. I was quite proud of myself for my efforts.

After a period of time, during our discussion, he suddenly turned to his son who had accompanied him into the examining room. In an annoyed tone he said, "Boinie, what's the matter mit dat doctor, can't he speak English?"

HOSPITAL JARGON

It was two AM in the morning when I received a call to see an elderly gentleman in the emergency room who had experienced severe heart failure. The patient had just arrived after a long flight from Israel. Mr. G was moving to the U.S. to live with his son during the later years of his life.

At this time, he spoke very little English and communicated with me in Hebrew and Russian through his son as an interpreter. The process was very time-consuming and I was not certain whether my questions were understood and properly answered. I finally decided to try to communicate directly with the patient by speaking Yiddish, hoping he could converse in that language. I was faced with a most difficult task with my limited vocabulary, but at least I could understand him.

He was delighted! Not only could I understand him, but his dialect was the same as my mother's, having come from the same area of Russia as my mother. What a relief for Mr. G, who just entered a new world without understanding the language nor his acute illness.

After his initial treatment, to which he made a good response, I arranged for him to be admitted to the hospital. He was most grateful. We shook hands and as I started to leave, he grabbed my arm. "Doctor," he said, "Do the nurses in the hospital speak Yiddish too?"

WHO IS CALLING?

When a young physician first starts his practice, he rarely can afford the luxury of a vacation. One summer, I had an opportunity to attend a medical meeting in New York, at a reasonable price. My wife and I were excited at last to get away for a few days from my work and our children.

After we arrived at the hotel, we received a phone call from a local physician in New York. "Hello, is this Dr. T? Welcome to New York. I want to take you and your wife out tomorrow evening for a dinner at the Four Seasons and to a Broadway show afterwards."

Wow, this is great, I thought to myself.

"By the way," he continued, "tell Ruth she doesn't have to dress up to any great extent."

I was baffled. "My wife's name is not Ruth."

"Isn't this Dr. Arnold T to whom I'm speaking?"

Sadly, I answered, "No, I am Dr. Herbert T. You must have the wrong number."

He realized that he was connected to the wrong room and apologized. In a disappointed voice, I wanted to answer before hanging up, "Gee, aren't you still going to take us out?"

WHAT DID YOU SAY?

Over the years, the sounds that penetrate our environment are constantly changing. The soft melodies of the past have been replaced by the loud rock music of the present. Speech content and volume have also fluctuated.

Mr. J, an elderly patient from the country, had lost his hearing thirty years previously. He would not make use of the advances made in the new sophisticated hearing aids. He was also unaware of the surgical procedures that could be applied to his type of hearing loss.

When he visited my office, I finally convinced Mr. J to undergo an operation for his disability. He at last, agreed.

After his recovery from the operation, with the restoration of his hearing, I asked, "Mr. J, how does it feel to hear once again after all these years?"

With a grim countenance, he replied, "You know Doc, to tell you the truth, there ain't nothin' worth listening to!"

I CAN PLAINLY SEE

Over the years, I have always enjoyed excellent vision without the need for glasses. A routine physical examination of a patient can sometimes yield some strange results about their eyesight.

One morning, I was examining a patient's eye grounds by means of an ophthalmoscope. In order to focus on a person's retina, the setting on the instrument must include a lens to correct the examiner's vision as well as the patient's. In my case, the setting normally is a negative three to allow me to clearly focus on the retina. I noted that with this patient, I had to use a much stronger correcting lens.

After the examination, I discussed the findings with the patient. I told her that she had a visual refraction error and should consult her ophthalmologist for a new set of glasses. "But Doctor," she replied, "I just had an eye exam last week and was told that I had perfect vision."

Conclusion: It was I who needed the eye examination and glasses!

Herbert L. Tanenbaum

SIMPLE ARITHMETIC

One of my patients, Professor K, told me about an encounter with the famous math genius, Dr. Albert Einstein. Dr. K was a prominent cellist with the Berlin Symphony Orchestra. On weekends, a group of professional musicians and an occasional amateur, would get together for an afternoon of performing chamber music. Albert Einstein often participated as an amateur violinist.

On one occasion, while playing with the group, Dr. Einstein was completely out of rhythm with the others. Finally, after a period of missed beats, Dr. K angrily pointed a finger at the math genius. "What is the matter with you, Albert? Don't you know how to count? One…! Two…! Three…!"

WORDS OF WISDOM

An aged patient arrived at the office for his annual physical examination. I always enjoyed his visit because of his wonderful sense of humor. We often exchanged quips and humorous stories.

Unfortunately, his health habits were not the best. After the examination, I spoke to him in my consultation room and listed all of the bad habits that affected his health—like smoking, lack of exercise, and poor diet.

After my long discourse, he replied, "You know, Doc," I notice that you yourself are growing old with me. You gave me a lot of advice, so let me leave you with advice of my own."

"One: Never pass by a urinal without using it!"

"Two: Never take an erection for granted!"

"Three: And never try to second guess a fart!"

The amazing thing was that he never charged me for his advice!

PART FIVE:
RELATIVELY SPEAKING

Herbert L. Tanenbaum

TAKE MY BAG, PLEASE!

Yea! I finally arranged for a weekend off. I had just started practice and was spending long hours setting up an office and caring for critically ill patients. My wife was busy caring for four children, including six-month-old twins, and we both needed the rest. My mother-in-law agreed to be the baby sitter.

Before taking off for our weekend in West Virginia, I reluctantly asked my wife if it was all right to stop by the hospital on our way out of town. I wanted to check on a very sick patient, although I had good coverage by another doctor. She agreed.

After arriving at the hospital, I said, "I will only be a few minutes." Every doctor's wife well knows that this estimation of time usually means at least a half-hour. I left her in the car. But after a time, she decided to go inside for a cup of coffee rather than wait any longer in the automobile.

Thirty minutes later, as she predicted, I came down and met her in the lobby. We got to the car to discover that someone had stolen our suitcase from the unlocked car!

My wife started to cry at the thought of a ruined week-end vacation. Angrily, I interjected that in no way would I let this misfortune spoil our trip. "Let's go to a nearby department store and buy all the clothes we will need, and off we'll go." This idea pleased her to no end.

West Virginia was beautiful with romantic music and gorgeous scenery. The weekend was most restful. Our lodge was simple and unadorned and situated far from the city. There wasn't even a drug store nearby or on the premises. On the way home, I bought a souvenir wooden planter bucket with a pine seed in the soil. (The word *pine tree* translates to *Tanenbaum* in German.) Each day it was to be watered and eventually it would sprout to a baby tree.

Out of the Doctor's Bag

After returning home, I conscientiously watered the soil and nothing grew. In the meantime, to our surprise, another seed, a different Tanenbaum, was growing in my wife's abdomen. We realized that our contraceptive jelly was stolen along with the suitcase. No drug store—and no protection.

Nine months later, we were blessed with a beautiful baby boy who has brought us such a great deal of joy and pleasure over the years.

Whoever stole our suitcase, please come forward to receive your reward!

IT IS GOD'S TURN

As a general rule, it is not prudent for a physician to treat his own family. Emotional factors often interfere with his judgment and decision making.

My father had suffered several strokes and was quite debilitated. He developed pneumonia, which is not unusual in his condition and which usually is a gentle terminal event.

In those days, patients, at that stage of their illness were more often cared for in their home environment. I was working as a medical resident at that time and would bring home intravenous fluids and antibiotics to treat his terminal illness.

Our family physician went along with me, probably more for my peace of mind rather than for any hope of my father's recovery. After several weeks of these frustrating, fruitless attempts to reverse the inevitable, Dr. H put his arm on my shoulder. "You know, one thing you have to learn as a physician is when to take your hands *off* the patient and let God put His hand *on* the patient"

Pop passed away peacefully without the extra needle sticks and IVs.

Out of the Doctor's Bag

MOTHERS CAN TELL

It is not unusual for a mother to bring her child to a physician and tell the doctor that the child is sick. After a thorough examination, sometimes no evidence of disease nor abnormalities are found. The mother still insists that something is wrong with her child. Several days later, the child has fever and other signs and symptoms. How did the mother know? Part of the answer is her keen observation of a slight behavioral change, a look in the child's eyes…or it is just plain mother's intuition?

One day, my mother called me to say that something was wrong with my older brother. "He just doesn't look right." The next day I did a thorough examination, with laboratory and X-ray studies and found nothing. He did not appear any different to me.

Well, Mom kept insisting there was something amiss with him and reprimanded me for not finding out what was wrong. Several weeks passed by and suddenly Joe came down with a high fever and confusion. I hospitalized him for further studies. I didn't tell Mom because she would have been extremely disturbed and distressed if she knew that he was sick enough to be in the hospital.

We finally established the diagnosis of a rare pituitary tumor that was fortunately benign. After his intercurrent infection and the endocrine disorder were treated, he made a satisfactory recovery and felt much better.

When he was discharged, my mother, not knowing that he had been in the hospital, called. "You know, Joe is looking much better now, even without your help."

I think, in the future, doctors should pay more attention to a mother's intuition.

Herbert L. Tanenbaum

NOW, THAT'S FUNNY!

Advanced Parkinson's Disease remains one of the horrors of our aging population. The illness is characterized by a paucity of movement, frozen facial features, and an inability to smile. Sometimes speech itself is rendered impossible.

My older brother, before his affliction with Parkinson's Disease, had the most keen sense of humor of anyone I have ever known. He would heartily laugh at someone else's jokes and tell his own with animation and style. During the last months of his life, he was a resident in a nursing home. He hadn't spoken nor smiled in months. In addition, he required tube feeding.

One day, my wife and I visited him. We tried to communicate with him. The only response we got was an expressionless stare. Finally, in frustration, with nothing else to say, my wife asked, "Joe, how do you like the food here?" This remark, which usually is a benign piece of conversation, was made as the unholy gray nourishing feeding was dripping into the tube placed in his stomach.

With what must have been an extreme effort on his part, Joe realized the humor of the remark, in view of the circumstances. He cracked a big smile for the first time in months. Sometimes, humor can be a very effective medicine.

THEY GO ON SALE NEXT WEEK

Humor comes in many forms. Sometimes it is associated with events that are less than humorous and occasionally tragic. On the positive side, a sense of humor often allows us to overcome or make more bearable unfortunate events that happen in our lives. In many instances, time may solve these problems.

I learned a great deal about the importance of patient humor when my mother was under my care. Throughout her life, she survived adversity and many mishaps with a keen sense of humor and a positive attitude that everything would work out for the better.

At the age of 85, she was afflicted with a cerebral vascular accident that resulted in an expressive speech aphasia. She retained her motor ability to speak, but could not attach a correct name to objects shown to her. Most patients with this deficit are depressed, cry easily and understandably experience great distress.

Each morning, I would test my mother by showing her different objects to name. A set of keys would be called "pens," a comb would be identified as a "pencil." She expressed less anxiety with these daily quizzes than I did. I was always anxiously looking for and hoping there would be some sign of improvement.

One day, I leaned over her bed and placed my neck tie in her hands. "Mom, what is this?"

She looked at the tie, felt it and with her usual smile and twinkle in her eye, she replied. "I don't know what it is, but can't you afford a better one?"

IF I HAD MY WAY

Over twenty years ago, my wife underwent a very serious operation. After her initial post-operative period, I arranged to have her transferred to the VIP suite of the hospital for her recuperation period. The room was very spacious, beautifully decorated with a tiled bathroom, sitting area, large dining room tables and chairs, large console TV, and a fully equipped kitchen. There was enough room for me to sleep over.

I wanted to impress my mother with how well I treated my wife. I took her to the hospital and to the suite, which was on the top floor of the hospital, and showed her around. She seemed quite awed with the surroundings and its amenities.

"Well, Mom, what do you think of all this?"

There was a pause and she finally replied in a thoughtful manner, "You know, better you should be in good health in the basement than sick in the penthouse!"

THANK YOU VERY MUCH

Wouldn't all of us like to know how we are feeling? If this question sounds strange, let me tell you about a favorite aunt of mine. She was quite a personality with no qualms about speaking her mind or asking questions.

One day, unfortunately, she fell and broke her leg. This accident required a prolonged hospitalization in those days.

Every day during her hospital stay, she would call the hospital front desk.

"Is this patient information?" she would ask. "I would like to know how Mrs. S (my aunt herself) is feeling today!"

The answer was the usual perfunctory reply to these inquiries. "Mrs. S is feeling fine and resting comfortably."

"Thank you very much." Mrs. S could then rest comfortably.

Herbert L. Tanenbaum

A.A.D. (ALSO A DOCTOR)

A favorite aunt of mine had quite a reputation for diagnosing and treating a variety of illnesses without the benefit of a medical degree. She never was shy about voicing her opinions about curative procedures and medication.

On one occasion, while was in the hospital with a broken leg, she refused traction of her leg and insisted that her bone would not 'knit' with the constant pulling of the traction.

Most of her diagnoses and cures were related to the gastrointestinal tract. When my father suffered a stroke, she insisted that a good bowel cleaning would clear his neurological deficit.

Another of her favorite activities was to write letters to well-known persons in order to advise them of solutions to their medical problems. Here is the letter she sent to actress Elizabeth Taylor.

Dear Miss Taylor,

I am writing because I read in the newspaper you are in the hospital with back problems. I am sorry that a beautiful girl such as yourself is sick so much.

My advice to you is to stay with your husband, Eddie Fisher, and stop going around with so many men. Your husband is a fine, handsome Jewish boy and certainly does not deserve all the trouble you cause him.

Maybe if you slept in your own bed with your sweet husband, your back wouldn't give you such pain.

Some medical school should have bestowed on her an honorary doctor of medicine degree or at least an A.A.D. (Also a Doctor.)

Out of the Doctor's Bag

A THIEF'S REWARD

One of the less aesthetic tasks a patient is asked to perform is to bring a fresh stool specimen to the laboratory or the office.

After a full week of diarrhea, my wife collected a stool sample to be submitted to her doctor for examination. Under the circumstances, she had no trouble in carrying out his instructions. An empty pickled herring jar was available for the specimen.

Off she went to the lab with her jar neatly packed in a department store bag which she placed on the front seat of her automobile. On her way, she decided to stop at the local cobbler to pick up some repaired shoes. When she returned to her car, lo and behold, someone had stolen the bag with its valuable "treasure" from the parked automobile.

Can you picture the look on the thief's face when he examined his *booty*?

PART SIX:
POTPOURRI

Herbert L. Tanenbaum

YOURS OR MINE?

Two elderly gentlemen were leaving the office one cold fall day. They were friends who had similar tastes in clothing. Each had an identical coat hanging on the coat rack. After putting on one of the coats, Mr. V started to leave.

Mr. W also took a coat off the rack, examined it and quickly turned to his friend. "Mr. V, you are wearing my coat! "You have put on the wrong one." Mr. V replied,

"You are wrong, Mr. W, this is my coat."

Well, the accusations went back and forth until Mr. W said, "Mr. V, put your hand into the right hand pocket of the coat you are wearing. What do you find?" Mr. V's hand came out of the pocket, clutching a set of keys. "You see," Mr. W continued, "those are my keys and that is my coat you're wearing!"

Mr. V stood quietly with a confused look on his face. How could this be? he thought to himself. There was only one answer. Only one defense. He turned to his friend and declared firmly, "Mr. W, what are your keys doing in my coat?"

Never give up!

Out of the Doctor's Bag

A PICTURE IS WORTH 1,000

A number of years ago, I had the pleasure of having lunch with one of the world's greatest medical illustrators. He shared this story with me while we ate.

As a young man, he was always interested in art and naturally took some lessons. His mother and older sister were concerned that he would not be able to earn a living in that field of drawing and painting. They discussed his potential with the art teacher. The instructor said that F did have unusual talent. So the two ladies made a compromise with their young man. If he would also attend medical school, they would go along with his art instruction.

Well, F graduated from medical school and finally opened an office for the practice of medicine. At that time, the country was in the midst of the depression and his practice consisted of only a handful of patients. He told me that the only professionals, in the field of health, that made a living during the depression were the veterinarians.

One day, apparently aware of his artistic ability, a drug firm commissioned him to draw twelve medical charts. He eagerly grabbed the opportunity in order to supplement his meagre income. After completing the assignment, the drug company asked him about his fees. Dr. F asked for $100. The company sent him a check for $1200, or one hundred dollars for each drawing. Dr. F had expected $100 for all twelve charts.

After he received the payment, Dr. F put a lock on his office door and went to work for the drug company, never to practice medicine again. His good fortune was also medicine's good fortune. His superb medical illustrations have continued to educate generations of physicians to the present day and into the foreseeable future.

GOD ACTS IN STRANGE WAYS

I've always been amazed at how critical experiences in times of stress will cause us to relate to a higher being. Mr. C, over the years, had distanced himself from any religious practices. As he was growing older, he decided to become more involved with his faith and started to attend synagogue services more regularly.

One Sabbath, while leaving the synagogue, he reached up, for good luck, to touch the mezuzah, (a religious object,) located on the side of the door. Just at that moment, the door swung open, caught his finger and he suffered a serious fracture.

Mr. C was taken to the emergency room of a nearby hospital where he required operative correction of the fracture. He suddenly experienced chest pain during the procedure. Mr. C suffered a heart attack and was immediately treated for this complication. He was admitted to the hospital and fortunately did quite well.

I was called to see him for the heart attack. He told me how his finger was broken by the synagogue door. I questioned him about his new-found belief in God in view of the misfortunes that had just happened to him. His immediate response was. "No, no, Doctor, God saved my life by allowing my finger to be broken. That way I was taken to the hospital where my heart attack occurred and I immediately received life-saving emergency treatment. The attack would have happened sooner or later outside of the hospital and I might not have survived."

A DILEMMA

Mrs. S was the wife of a very prominent public figure and was also quite affluent. Unfortunately, she was afflicted with an unusual congenital, inherited disease characterized by tell-tale marks on the lips and skin. Gastrointestinal bleeding from these lesions in the intestinal tract is also a hallmark of the condition.

Over the years, I learned a great deal about her family history and the birthplace of her parents before they came to America. They had resided in a small town in Russia that had a strange sounding name.

One day, I was asked by a social service agency if I would make a house call on an indigent patient in a poor section of town. He was apparently bleeding from his bowel and could not afford a doctor.

I agreed and drove to the run-down apartment where he lived in humble surroundings. The first thing I noticed were the tell-tale marks on his lips and ears. The cause of the intestinal bleeding and the congenital abnormality were the same as Mrs. S. When I asked the gentleman his name, it corresponded with the maiden name of Mrs. S, with the same spelling. The wheels were turning in my mind at these similarities. "Where were your parents from…? I named the Russian village where Mrs. S's parents originated.

He nearly fell off his chair. "How did you know?" he replied. "I haven't heard that name since I was a boy!" There was no question in my mind that the two patients were closely related, probably cousins.

One day, they were sitting in my office waiting room at the same time. What should I do? Do I introduce them and potentially create a problem for both, one being poor and destitute and the other famous and wealthy. Where could I find an answer to this dilemma?

Herbert L. Tanenbaum

HER LUCKY DAY

During the gasoline crisis, I drove to a nearby station and waited in line. I glanced out of my window to the left and suddenly noticed a large car backing up toward the side of my car. I could not move forward or backward because I was in the middle of the line. I started to blow my horn and yelled out of the window, to no avail. The car slowly crunched into the side of my car, leaving a large dent.

The female driver came out of her car. I was preparing to exchange insurance information. We looked at each other, and I was astonished to see that she was one of my patients.

There was no apology, and the first thing she said, with a happy tone to her voice, was, "Dr. T, am I glad I ran into you! I was about to call you with some questions I have about my medications."

FROM THE CRADLE TO THE GRAVE

Certain images, although fleeting and very simplistic in form, can convey a great deal of meaning and thought.

One day, as I was leaving the hospital, I took the elevator down from the top floor to the ground floor entrance. Two stops were made on the way down. One was at the obstetric floor where a mother and her new born infant got on. At the next stop, an orderly pushed a stretcher on the elevator. It carried a draped, recently expired patient being taken down to the morgue.

I looked at the baby and observed a little pink, soft and warm infant's hand with a clenched first. He seemed to be grabbing and holding on to everything that life can offer.

Another hand protruded from under the sheets of the gurney. That hand was white and cold with an outstretched open palm. It was leaving behind everything that life had offered, taking nothing with him.

The image of these adjacent hands tells the story of life better than a thousand words.

Herbert L. Tanenbaum

TAXI, PLEASE!

How often do we experience what seems to be a minor event only to learn later that it made the difference between life or death?

Mr. R. was enjoying a vacation on his boat off the coast of Florida. Suddenly, he was seized with severe, pressing chest pains and shortness of breath. He realized that he needed medical attention. Fortunately, the boat was close to shore, near Miami, where he docked. He considered calling for an emergency ambulance, but instead, hailed a cab passing by. He told the driver to take him to a hospital across town, one that he was familiar with.

During the ride, the cabby looked through the rear view mirror and realized that his passenger was feeling poorly and looked ashen.

"Excuse me, Sir," said the cabby, "it seems to me that you look pretty sick. How 'bout if I take you to a hospital much closer to where we are?" Mr. R reluctantly agreed.

After arriving at the emergency room, Mr. R paid the cabby and walked in.

Suddenly, at the entrance, he collapsed and went into cardiac arrest. The staff successfully resuscitated him without any residual effects. Later he underwent an urgent coronary by-pass operation at that hospital, well known for this procedure. He was discharged in a few days in good condition and was referred to me when he returned to Washington.

Does anyone know this alert cabby whose clear perception saved my patient's life?

Out of the Doctor's Bag

WITH A PICKLE, OF COURSE!

There are certain things that just can't wait. These include a before-dinner cocktail, a cigarette for those who smoke, and a good lunch.

Mr. T was admitted to the hospital with a history of recurrent chest pain and was to undergo diagnostic heart catheterization in order to study his coronary arteries.

A hospital stay of any length, affords the physician the opportunity to instruct and to teach a patient the benefits of a low-fat diet, exercise, and other strategies for maintaining good health.

In the afternoon, I was making hospital rounds and noted a strange smell that was not normally part of the usual hospital aromas. It was familiar and most pleasant.

At that moment, Mr. T was being wheeled out of the catheterization laboratory and I accompanied him into his room. There at his side, on the stretcher, was a brown bag. The bag contained a corned beef sandwich on rye bread with a kosher pickle!

In spite of the fat content of the meat, I had to admit there certainly was a welcome change from the usual hospital smell of antiseptics.

WE NEVER GROW UP

Even as we grow into adults, become educated and sophisticated and trained in our profession, we can never completely free ourselves from the apron strings of our mother.

A young woman was undergoing a complex surgical repair of a congenital heart defect in a well-known cardiac surgical unit. She was anesthetized and connected to the newly developed heart-lung, perfusion pump. The operation was going smoothly when all of a sudden all hell broke loose.

The tubing from the patient to the heart perfusion pump broke loose and spurts of blood flooded the operating room. As if this wasn't enough, her heart rhythm became erratic and a marked drop in blood pressure ensued. Calm heads addressed the situation and corrected the mishaps. The patient responded and eventually made a full recovery. Later, I asked the surgeon, a good friend and superb surgeon, "Charley, what was in your mind when all those mishaps and problems came up during the operation?"

"You know," he said, "I was only hoping my mother was coming to pick me up!"

PART SEVEN:
Requiem

Herbert L. Tanenbaum

MALVERN MARTIN HAS PASSED AWAY

The adage of "Do unto others as you would have others do unto you" is not followed in every instance.

One memorable patient, Malvern Martin, fifty-five years old, was a member of several church, charitable and fraternal organizations. One of his volunteer jobs, which he took great pride in, was to write brief obituaries for departing members and to submit them to the organization's newsletters and to local newspapers. He performed his duties well and would often read and show me the finished articles that he carried in his wallet.

He had no children and was married to an elderly and very ill woman. Malvern would bring her to the office, help her to the examining room and then show my receptionist the latest obituary he had written.

As fate would have it, one day Mr. Martin unexpectedly passed away. Each day I would read the obituary columns of the local papers looking for his obituary. Time went by and to my surprise and not without a note of sadness, no one ever bothered to write his obit! I will!

Malvern Martin has passed away.

Out of the Doctor's Bag

REQUIEM

I hope you have enjoyed my recounting of so many memorable experiences I have had in the practice of medicine over the past 43 years. Some of these are humorous, some sad and a few with messages of hope and words to live by.

I would like to close with passages from a letter written to me by a dying patient during her last days. She expresses the joys of living, not the fear of dying, with such simple eloquence.

The truth is, it is hard to believe I may be dying. I continue with daily chores, like watering the plants, marking changes of address in a notebook, or even cutting out new recipes. I try to think about not being, but I am not successful. My mind turns to the outdoors, to buying fresh fish for the next meal, to my need for a new pair of yard shoes. I enjoy clipping back the geraniums, fertilizing the flower bed, or simply enjoying another spring and summer. Riding across the marshlands of Florida last May, we saw a colony of wood storks near a bed of water hyacinths and what looked like a white heron hatchery, the babies with their mothers grouped like any family gathering for a picnic. Wild yellow irises grew in the ditches with heavy nodding flowers, thistle, too, not so large or fat as those in Northern fields but in clusters of rich color.

This, I thought, it is what I enjoy. It is what I have always enjoyed most. I need little more "to pleasure myself" as they say in the South. Then why had I spent so much time folding mail for a politician whose ethics I didn't really know, worked for planned parenthood, put in time at bridge, backgammon, word games, and luncheons with people who spent their lives putting in time?

Herbert L. Tanenbaum

As a child, in the spring, each morning I looked to see whether our lilac bush, which almost reached my window, was budding early. I followed its progress each day as a mother watches her child the first year, aroused by the fragrance of fresh bread baking in our kitchen, I would dress for school, but I did not like the classroom. I preferred to be outside, to feel the breeze and walk in the woods. At the end of our street was a piece of virgin forest where we played. Violets in blue profusion bloomed there so thick we walked on them while we picked bouquets. A stream trickled down to a creek where we found flint arrowheads and other artifacts. We studied them and left them where they rested. None of us had the collector's instinct.

It was a beautiful world for a child. It is beautiful to me now, with all its troubles, wars and hatreds. I tell myself that if, with a failing heart, I can still enjoy all that is good around me—springtime, the pretty children, blue sky, the songs of the mocking bird that nests near our front porch, I shall have taken something of heaven with me when I die.

Although I have had more than my share of illness and family tragedies, the effect was that we did learn to appreciate the good times between the bad. For me—unlike the homeless, the starving, the angry, the massacred, those who labor all their lives and never glimpse the sea or other beauty of this earth, who never have a chance to leave their narrow alley world, to think in fresh categories, to explore, to run on the wind—for me it was a good life. And I wish everyone to know I am grateful.

ABOUT THE AUTHOR

Dr. Herbert L. Tanenbaum, M.D., F.A.C.P., F.A.C.C., is a board certified internist and cardiologist. He has been in the practice of medicine in the District of Columbia and Maryland for 43 years. In addition to his private medical practice, he has been involved in research, teaching and administration. His hospital experiences have been at university, municipal, private and research institutions.

www.ingramcontent.com/pod-product-compliance
Lightning Source LLC
Chambersburg PA
CBHW032021040426
42448CB00006B/690